THE VERBAL ABUSE RECOVERY JOURNAL

The Verbal Abuse Recovery

Journal

Prompts and Practices for Healing

Stephanie Sandoval, LMFT

ROCKRIDGE
PRESS

Series Designer: Karmen Lizzul
Interior and Cover Designer: Scott Petrower
Art Producer: Tom Hood
Editor: Brian Sweeting
Production Editor: Emily Sheehan
Production Manager: Martin Worthington

Illustration © SpiffyJ/iStock, 2021. Author photograph courtesy Kome Parnell/KP Imagery by Design.

Paperback ISBN 978-1-64876-477-6
R0

CONTENTS

When I dare to be powerful, to use my strength in the service of my vision, then it becomes less and less important whether I am afraid.

—AUDRE LORDE

INTRODUCTION

Welcome to a space of support, guided introspection, and self-reclamation. I am so grateful you are here because you matter, your safety matters, and your well-being matters. May this journal greet you exactly as you are, wherever you are in time.

My name is Stephanie Sandoval, and I am a licensed marriage and family therapist and founder of Collective Space Therapy. I have spent years providing individualized and integrative therapy for adults, and advocating for the availability of mental health services for all people and communities. I am passionate about supporting individuals on their personal journeys of self-exploration, reflection, and development through therapy. Extensive training and clinical work with individuals experiencing low self-esteem, depression, and trauma have allowed me to develop a creative approach to therapy with a humanistic lens.

I first became focused on the topic of verbal abuse when I began addressing my own personal struggles with mental health during my years of mentoring. In my adolescence, I experienced verbal abuse from my mother as an outcome of an authoritarian parenting style, which is common in the Latinx culture. As I began my career, I became empowered by adopting an anti oppressive framework. As my relationship with my mother began to mend in my adult life, my work naturally gravitated toward intergenerational healing. I became an impassioned advocate for fostering education, self-reflection, connection, and compassion as they relate to the cultural, sociopolitical, and diverse needs of each individual.

Verbal abuse occurs in a variety of forms, but it can be categorized as use of language and other forms of verbal communication that cause physical discomfort, mental stress, and emotional harm. Verbal aggression can be difficult to identify, but it is the communication equivalent of throwing a punch—the intent is to induce a desired emotional response (Carney & Neuhart, 2020). Also known as verbal bullying or emotional intimidation, this form of abuse is an act of using disrespectful, insulting, and harsh language to gain or maintain power and control. Whether a conscious or unconscious act on the part of the abuser, it is never acceptable. Examples of verbal aggression are belligerent behavior such as yelling, screaming, swearing, name-calling, and making threats and accusations. Similarly, relational aggression includes inflicting emotional pain through social isolation (the absence of contact between a person and others), group exclusion (the absence of contact between a person and others that is due to external factors, such as force or another person's manipulation), and manipulation of relationships (Lefler & Hartung, 2017). More covert forms of verbal abuse include gaslighting, constant correcting, belittling remarks, demeaning comments, and prolonged silent treatment.

Anyone can experience verbal abuse, whether from friends, family, colleagues, or romantic partners. Those who have experienced verbal abuse or who have witnessed its exchange in their youth can often overlook it; they may have internalized verbal abuse as an acceptable way to communicate (Rizvi, 1969). Unfortunately, this can have lasting detrimental effects on one's mental health. The person on the receiving end of verbal abuse may feel an abundance of complex emotions, such as fear, anxiety, insecurity, rejection, humiliation, frustration, shame, guilt, and confusion. It is common for victims to believe the abuse is a result of something they did wrong or that it might even be deserved because of who they are. It is important to learn and understand that no one deserves verbal abuse—and no one is immune.

The process of recovering from verbal abuse will look unique to each individual, and this guided journal can provide a helpful pathway of what to expect. There is no right or wrong way to heal, nor is there a time limit. Modern society often demands quick fixes and instant gratification, but the reality of recovery is that it requires patience, pure intent, and an appetite for long-term perspective. Healing is not linear, and you'll need to expect ups and downs, and accept the possibility of momentary setbacks.

The recommendation is to work through the journal from beginning to end, but feel free to use this resource in whichever way works best for you. DBT, dialectical behavior therapy, is an evidenced-based comprehensive cognitive behavioral treatment that is referred to throughout the journal. It focuses on strategies like mindfulness, acceptance, and emotion regulation. While this journal is an excellent way to work through a variety of different topics, any ongoing or debilitating symptoms of anxiety, depression, trauma, and other mental health concerns should be addressed by a medical professional as soon as possible. If you recognize any complicated emotions or feelings that could lead to you harming yourself or others, please seek immediate assistance and call 911. This journal is not a replacement for a therapist, medication, or medical treatment. There is absolutely no shame in seeking help or treatment. You are not alone, and you are infinitely worthy of support.

I wish to acknowledge the profound bravery it takes to enter this new territory. Treading into the discomfort of the unknown for the sake of truth is courageous. You are the hero of your own story. You have suffered from the pain of verbal abuse, and you are now admirably taking the steps toward healing and empowerment. By using this journal as an opportunity to explore a deeper understanding of yourself, you will gain a greater introspection regarding your past, awareness of your present, and an expanded vision for your future. I commend you for embarking on this daring new life chapter and building a strong foundation to hold the vastness of all that you are and who you will become.

PART 1

ACKNOWLEDGE THE WOUND

When we own the story, we can write a brave new ending.

—BRENÉ BROWN

When we're faced with verbal and emotional abuse, denial is often our first line of defense. It's a survival tactic to conceal wounds that cannot be fully understood until safety is found. The act of reckoning with denial is, in certain ways, a difficult concession that the wound exists. It can be genuinely terrifying, and feelings of confusion, anxiousness, shame, self-consciousness, and uncertainty can bubble up. It's a painful admission of victimhood, an announcement to one's self that harm has been done.

The relationship we have with ourselves is foundational, and not acknowledging pain can have profound effects on our lives. In the short term, this includes overwhelming feelings of hopelessness. In the long term, it can manifest itself into anxiety and depression. This section will assist you with acknowledging the wound and allowing you to gain acceptance, an emergence of clarity, and an increased capacity for resilience as you reclaim yourself.

When we acknowledge the wound, we enter into an intimate yet terrifying new territory. We are facing a sacred monster within our inner world. As we explore a deeper part of ourselves, emotional intelligence is a key foundation in the journey toward healing and recovery. What did your family, culture, and society teach you about emotions and feelings? What feelings are you uncomfortable showing others? Think back to your childhood, and reflect on how those feelings were handled when you showed them.

Having a safe space is vital in this process of recovery. Write about your safe space and what it looks like. How can you access it? What does it represent to you?

_____

_____

_____

_____

_____

_____

_____

_____

_____

_____

_____

_____

_____

_____

_____

As you acknowledge your wound, you recognize being a victim. Write about something negative that comes to mind when you think about a victim and/or being a victim— something you know realistically is not true. Why isn't it true? Ask yourself who put this view in your mind.

_____

_____

_____

_____

_____

_____

_____

_____

_____

_____

_____

_____

_____

_____

_____

_____

Emotions are core dimensions to the human experience. Although the words "emotions" and "feelings" are used interchangeably, they are distinct: emotions are associated with sensations activated in the body through neurotransmitters and hormones released by the brain, and feelings are the conscious experience of emotional reactions that we can name. It's imperative to learn that feelings aren't facts but information, and are neither "good" nor "bad." Paul Ekman has dedicated his career to researching emotions, focusing primarily on these seven basic emotions (Ekman, 2007):

Feeling	Information
Fear	Danger lurks
Sadness	Impending loss
Anger	An urgent plea for justice and action
Joy	Impending gain
Surprise	Unexpected event
Disgust	Contamination, toxic contact
Contempt	Substandard behavior or being

Think about each feeling, and write down the emotional sensations that come to mind when you have experienced each feeling in the past.

When I feel fear, I experience these emotional sensations in my body:

_____

_____

When I feel sadness, I experience these emotional sensations in my body:

_____

_____

When I feel anger, I experience these emotional sensations in my body:

_____

_____

When I feel joy, I experience these emotional sensations in my body:

_____

_____

When I feel disgust, I experience these emotional sensations in my body:

_____

_____

When I feel contempt, I experience these emotional sensations in my body:

_____

_____

How has the stigma surrounding mental health, including societal disapproval and negative perceptions of people who struggle with mental health, prevented you from fully acknowledging your wound? Write about how the stigma has influenced your thoughts, beliefs, and behaviors. What are you holding on to that is keeping you from healing yourself fully? How can you move toward releasing this from your reality?

_____

_____

_____

_____

_____

_____

_____

_____

_____

_____

_____

_____

_____

_____

_____

Verbal abuse might not leave physical cuts and bruises, but the emotional scars are deep. Feelings are colorful, complicated, and fascinating, and they provide context to the human experience. Sometimes feelings can be complex because you can experience multiple feelings at once. Pain, when examined, becomes clarity. Think about a recent event or experience with verbal abuse that seems to have stuck in your mind no matter what. What are three feelings that you could use to describe your experience?

_____

_____

_____

_____

_____

_____

_____

_____

_____

_____

_____

_____

Acknowledging the deep pain from verbal abuse can lead to feelings of fear, stimulating the nervous system and causing a fight-flight-freeze-fawn reaction. Fear tells you that you're unsafe. It can arise as a protective response to past trauma. It's important to recognize these responses in a safe space. In fight mode, we move toward the threat with aggression; in flight mode, we quickly move away from the threat; in freeze mode, we silently shut down in front of the threat; and in fawn mode, we move toward the threat, trying to please them to avoid conflict. Write down what reactions you can identify with.

_____

_____

_____

_____

_____

_____

_____

_____

_____

_____

_____

_____

_____

Body scanning involves paying close attention to parts of the body and bodily sensations in a gentle and gradual sequence, starting with the toes and concluding with the top of the head. As you become more aware of your body's sensations, you can better identify the emotions you experience from moment to moment. Practice this body-scan exercise regularly as a tool to identify emotions.

BODY SCAN

1. Close your eyes.
2. Scan your body.
3. Identify bodily sensations.
4. Name the emotion(s).

If you're feeling uncomfortable or overwhelmed, a body-scan meditation can help you focus on active tension points and release excess energy, restoring a sense of emotional regulation and calmness within. Find a quiet space with minimal distractions to practice the following exercise. Practice this meditation regularly, and use it as a coping tool when you're in distress.

BODY-SCAN MEDITATION

1. Get grounded—become present in your body, and connect with the earth through your sense of balance.
2. Take five deep breaths.
3. Bring attention to your toes.
4. Scan your body.
5. Bring attention to tension.
6. Breath deeply into the tension.

The curious paradox is that when I accept
myself just as I am, then I can change.
—CARL ROGERS

A crucial indicator of verbal abuse is toxic shame. Healthy shame is an emotion that lets us know we've made a mistake by doing something that doesn't align with our values. Toxic shame is an induced emotion that tells you that *you* are a mistake—a belief that causes inner conflict, self-blame, and low self-esteem. Projection is a defense mechanism that abusers commonly use; they project their unconscious feelings of shame and inadequacy that they are too uncomfortable to acknowledge onto a vulnerable and empathetic person, and these feelings are then internalized in that person as toxic shame. Describe your experience of toxic shame and how you can challenge those untrue beliefs.

Feelings of toxic shame are often paired with a loud inner critic. This voice criticizes you in a harsh tone with rude words. When you make a mistake, what does your inner critic tell you that you know is not true? How can you challenge this voice when it claims a mistake as evidence that you're an inadequate person?

_____

_____

_____

_____

_____

_____

_____

_____

_____

_____

_____

_____

_____

_____

Healing becomes easier when you share. An important step in this process is to share your experience with someone you trust in a safe space. This can be anyone in your life who has the capacity to emotionally support you without giving any advice—just to be there with you as a witness. A licensed therapist is highly recommended, as are survivor support groups. Think about sharing your story with a witness. What feelings and thoughts are coming up? Who comes to mind?

_____

_____

_____

_____

_____

_____

_____

_____

_____

_____

_____

_____

Identifying feelings is foundational to self-regulation. "Name it to tame it," a phrase created by psychiatrist Dr. Daniel Siegel, is a powerful tool that puts you in the driver's seat of your emotional world. When we deny feelings or have feelings about our feelings, our emotions can become stronger and last longer. When we name a feeling, it reengages our prefrontal cortex, and we begin to think more clearly. Once we name it to tame it, "a space is created to cope with overwhelming emotions" (Siegel & Bryson, 2016).

Make a list of feelings you've recently experienced:

_____

_____

_____

_____

_____

Once you name a feeling, think about how you can cope with the emotion and connect with the nurturing part of yourself by using each of your five senses in times of distress. An important reminder for this exercise: growth and distress can exist at the same time. Write down activities for each sense and practice them as grounding tools.

Smell: *e.g., finding a scent that calms you*

_____

_____

Touch: *e.g., wrapping yourself in a soft blanket*

_____

_____

Taste: *e.g., chewing your favorite gum*

_____

_____

Hearing: *e.g., playing your favorite song*

_____

_____

Sight: *e.g., watching your favorite movie*

_____

_____

Verbal abuse might not leave physical cuts and bruises, but the emotional scars are deep. Sometimes feelings can be complex because you can experience multiple feelings at once (for example, pain, when examined becomes clarity). Think about a recent event or experience with verbal abuse that seems to stick in the back of your mind no matter what. What was it? Identify three feelings you felt at the time. How do you feel after reflecting on it? What thoughts come to mind?

_____

_____

_____

_____

_____

_____

_____

_____

_____

_____

_____

_____

_____

Grieving the end of an abusive relationship can be complicated; you're grieving not only the end of the relationship, but a part of yourself that believed you had control. Think about the part of you that helped you survive in the relationship. What did you believe, and how did these beliefs influence your behavior? As you recognize this during your healing process, what new beliefs can you adopt as you recover?

_____

_____

_____

_____

_____

_____

_____

_____

_____

_____

_____

_____

_____

_____

Grief has no timetable. Overwhelming emotions can become intrusive. It can be cathartic to surrender to your feelings, but life and responsibilities can become a distraction. Scheduling grief is a useful way to compartmentalize your pain and increase your confidence in managing emotions. Putting this tool into practice, you can validate feelings that start to surface while gently reminding yourself that you have a sacred time for your grief to be fully seen and honored with the attention it deserves. If you could carve out time for your grief, what would that look like in your current schedule?

When you acknowledge the wound, you acknowledge something sacred–something that needs to be honored, protected, and cared for. You may feel like you've hit rock bottom and can't see a way up. I assure you, there is a light at the end of this tunnel, because you can grow and still have pain. This is a part of the process, and you are not alone. When you're experiencing painful emotions from the wound, art can be a wonderful outlet for expression and way to find your own meaning of pain. Create a collage or drawing that depicts your wound.

As you courageously face the pain of what you've been through, an empowered sense of self is born. By honoring your wound, dismantling conditioned beliefs that have outlived their time, and becoming confident in feeling your feelings, you have shown yourself how incredibly resilient you are—which is something to be proud of. With acceptance comes freedom. This is the end of a chapter in your life story. You're now ready to start a new chapter with a new narrative. What title would you give this new chapter in your healing? Imagine how this new chapter would look.

_____

_____

_____

_____

_____

_____

_____

_____

_____

_____

_____

_____

I am worth protecting.
My pain matters.

PART 2

ESTABLISH BOUNDARIES TO PROTECT YOURSELF

Boundaries make freedom possible.

—ROBERT AUGUSTUS MASTERS

As you begin to process the abuse you experienced, you can access a new sense of self-empowerment through an awareness of your needs and values. When you focus inward, you give yourself the space needed to heal through setting boundaries with abusers. Boundaries are sacred spaces that protect and assert our autonomy as individuals. They allow us to define who we are and whom we allow into our world. Boundaries can be a vital tool in determining how you separate your thoughts, feelings, and emotions from those of others. In developing healthy boundaries, only you can provide the inner safety you personally need—no one else can do that for you.

It can be an uncomfortable experience at first, but as you integrate boundary-setting into your life, you take back the power of self and protect yourself from further abuse. This section will help.

Family of origin plays a significant, and often critical, role in mental health. Think about your childhood and adolescent years. What boundaries existed in your homelife? Were they too rigid, too loose, or nonexistent? Were they consistent or inconsistent? What messages did your family give you regarding their beliefs around boundaries?

_____

_____

_____

_____

_____

_____

_____

_____

_____

_____

_____

_____

_____

_____

_____

What beliefs have you internalized that have created feelings of guilt when you think about setting boundaries? (For example: boundaries will threaten my relationships; boundaries will be unacceptable to others; boundaries are selfish, etc.)

_____

_____

_____

_____

_____

_____

_____

_____

_____

_____

_____

_____

_____

_____

What new beliefs can empower you and support you in feeling confident when you set boundaries in the future? (For example: boundaries are a form of self-respect; boundaries will help me heal; boundaries will help me build self-esteem, etc.)

_____

_____

_____

_____

_____

_____

_____

_____

_____

_____

_____

_____

_____

_____

_____

_____

As you begin learning about boundaries, it's crucial to first identify your fears. Write down five fears that come to mind. Revisit this prompt later and write down more fears as they pop into your head throughout your healing journey. As you continue the recovery process, review your fears and challenge them in a validating and supportive way.

_____

_____

_____

_____

_____

_____

_____

_____

_____

_____

_____

_____

_____

Healing from abuse requires you to reexamine your values as you strengthen your sense of identity. Boundaries help you live your values so you can connect with your inner truth. Values are our hearts' desires for how we want to interact with and relate to the world, others, and ourselves. Write down 15 values that come to mind. Remember that not everyone has the same values, and this isn't a test.

1. _____

2. _____

3. _____

4. _____

5. _____

6. _____

7. _____

8. _____

9. _____

10. _____

11. _____

12. _____

13. _____

14. _____

15. _____

What was it like for you to write down your values? Write down your thoughts, how you feel, and emotions you're experiencing.

_____

_____

_____

_____

_____

_____

_____

_____

_____

_____

_____

_____

_____

_____

_____

Sometimes our values aren't aligned with what is right for us. Our society, culture, family, and other factors may have been very influential in our formative years, causing us to internalize values that are not necessarily our own. Write down what your society values. What does your culture value? What did your family value? Which values did you internalize? Examine the relationship between these values to create clarity around, and insight into, limiting beliefs you may have adopted in life.

_____

_____

_____

_____

_____

_____

_____

_____

_____

_____

_____

_____

_____

_____

An important step in discovering your authentic values is learning about intrinsic and extrinsic values. Intrinsic values are inherently rewarding to pursue, and extrinsic values are centered on external approvals or rewards (Kahneman & Tversky, 2017). Understanding this distinction can help you gain clarity around the directions you keep moving in. Use the following list to identify intrinsic values, and fill in the blank spaces with additional intrinsic values that you currently have. Rank them from 1 to 10 in order of importance to you. Keep in mind that there are no right or wrong values.

Intrinsic values, values that are inherently rewarding to pursue:

_____ *Affiliation with friends and family*

_____ *Connection with nature*

_____ *Concern for others*

_____ *Self-acceptance*

_____ *Social justice*

_____ *Creativity*

_____ _____

_____ _____

_____ _____

_____ _____

Emotional self-defense . . . When you set healthier relationship standards in your life, some people will take it personally. That's their issue, not yours. The distance isn't against them; it's for you. It's a boundary, not a grudge.

—STEVE MARABOLI

When do you need boundaries? Focus on your emotions and listen to your feelings. When you recognize your emotions, you can use this information to determine how you feel. Where in your life do you neglect your own feelings in an attempt to manage someone else's? Where do you expect others to neglect their feelings to manage your feelings?

_____

_____

_____

_____

_____

_____

_____

_____

_____

_____

_____

_____

Once you focus on your emotional world, you can name the feeling and tame it by giving it the power of your attention. When you notice uncomfortable emotions arising, it might be a clear indication that your boundaries have been violated. You may notice your body getting tense and heated, allowing you to convey verbally that you're feeling angry. As you heal the wound of emotional abuse, your relationship with anger will change. How would you describe your current relationship with anger? How has your upbringing influenced the way you relate to anger?

_____

_____

_____

_____

_____

_____

_____

_____

_____

_____

_____

_____

As a victim of verbal abuse, you may feel anger toward yourself rather than toward the abuser when you feel you are being disrespected. Think about a time when you experienced verbal abuse and felt angry at yourself. Describe the situation, how it made you feel at the time, and what you thought. Then write about how you consider the situation now, using feelings as information.

_____

_____

_____

_____

_____

_____

_____

_____

_____

_____

_____

_____

_____

_____

It's normal to feel confusion, shame, and guilt when you first start setting boundaries. Knowing that boundaries convey your right to be an individual, separate from others, can help redirect any spiraling thoughts you may experience. Learn, know, and believe the rights you have as a human being. Write down these rights on a piece of paper. Stand tall in front of a mirror, and silently read each right. Then look up at yourself and repeat each confidently out loud to yourself. Repeat as many times as you like.

I have the right to be treated with respect.

I have the right to my own opinions.

I have the right to express my feelings.

I have the right to stand up for my values.

I have the right to disagree with others.

I have the right to ask for information.

I have the right to understand a request before agreeing to it.

I have the right to say no without guilt.

I have the right to ask for my wants and needs.

I have the right to set healthy boundaries with others.

I have the right to disengage from conflict.

When establishing boundaries, you'll need to know your physical, emotional, and mental limits. Our boundaries are the gatekeepers for what we say yes and no to, and mastering this skill takes time. Saying no to someone can seem incredibly daunting, especially when we want to please others. Write down your thoughts and feelings about saying no and setting limits with others. Where do you think this part of you came from? How can you challenge this?

_____

_____

_____

_____

_____

_____

_____

_____

_____

_____

_____

_____

_____

_____

Abusers frequently use passive, passive-aggressive, and aggressive communication in relationships. This can leave victims vulnerable to accepting the shame abusers project on them—shame that has resulted from their own unprocessed pain. When setting a boundary, use "I" statements to affirm your separateness. An "I" statement is a form of assertive communication, and it looks like this:

I feel <u>scared</u> when <u>you are yelling</u>, and I would <u>prefer that you speak to me in a lower voice so I can hear what you have to say</u>.

Think about a situation that made you feel angry, sad, and afraid to practice "I" statements. When you're done, reflect on your feelings and thoughts about this exercise.

1. *I feel* _____ *when* _____ *, and I would prefer* _____
_____.

2. *I feel* _____ *when* _____ *, and I would prefer* _____
_____.

3. *I feel* _____ *when* _____ *, and I would prefer* _____
_____.

4. *I feel* _____ *when* _____ *, and I would prefer* _____
_____.

5. *I feel* _____ *when* _____ *, and I would prefer* _____
_____.

When you're setting boundaries, it's important to be mindful of your presentation and to appear confident. Consider your body language and tone when conveying your message. Write down what might help you stay grounded and appear confident when you're being assertive.

_____

_____

_____

_____

_____

_____

_____

_____

_____

_____

_____

_____

_____

Think about a past situation when you felt compassionate toward someone who was verbally abusive to you. Understand that you couldn't set boundaries because you didn't know what they were. Now write a letter to your past self in a warm and supportive manner. How would you validate your past feelings in a supportive way? How would you let your past self know it's possible to feel compassionate and hold firm boundaries at the same time? What kind of words of encouragement would you use?

_____

_____

_____

_____

_____

_____

_____

_____

_____

_____

_____

_____

If you've experienced ongoing verbal abuse, feeling compassion can seem like second nature. Compassion is a gentle kindness without any conditions—it's a feeling letting you know that you understand the pain of another person and want to help. Often, feeling compassion can overshadow feelings of righteous anger, causing boundaries to loosen or become nonexistent. Big hearts need even bigger boundaries. An important step in setting boundaries is understanding that you can have both compassion and firm boundaries at the same time. You can feel compassion and anger. How is it for you to experience compassion? Write about a situation in which feeling compassionate did more harm than good.

_____

_____

_____

_____

_____

_____

_____

_____

_____

_____

_____

_____

I understand the power of boundaries, and as I set them with others, I am advocating for and honoring my authentic self.

PART 3

SHOW YOURSELF COMPASSION

Of all the judgments we pass in life, none is more important than the judgment we pass on ourselves.

—NATHANIEL BRANDEN

Compassion and kindness toward oneself are fundamental to the journey of healing. Recognize that to remain standing after enduring immense hardship and deprivation is a true testament to your resilience and strength.

So how do you respond to yourself when you're struggling? Responding with self-criticism and self-judgment is not uncommon. Through creating consciousness, however, we can create the space needed to observe ourselves, revealing our inner thoughts and feelings.

This section will help you become your own greatest ally. By reducing self-criticism, releasing what you cannot change, and achieving a sense of liberation, you'll learn how to support yourself when you face challenging moments. Awareness of our inner critic lets us speak to ourselves as if we're confiding in a loved one. Remember you are worthy of grace and gentleness through the ebbs and flows of pain.

You might not have been taught to have compassion for yourself. Think back to your childhood, and write about your early experiences with self-compassion. What negative beliefs come to mind when you think about self-compassion? Where did those come from? Now that you know the importance of self-compassion, what new beliefs can you adopt that will support you in your recovery?

_____

_____

_____

_____

_____

_____

_____

_____

_____

_____

_____

_____

_____

_____

Observing those who model compassion to others can be helpful in cultivating compassion for yourself. Think about a person or figure who embodies compassion. Who is it? Write down five traits they have that you admire and appreciate, and note what you'd like to emulate.

_____

_____

_____

_____

_____

_____

_____

_____

_____

_____

_____

_____

_____

_____

Seeing a close friend or loved one in pain can bring forth many different kinds of feelings and thoughts. How do you usually respond to people you care about when they are suffering? Think about what you feel, what you think, and what you say.

_____

_____

_____

_____

_____

_____

_____

_____

_____

_____

_____

_____

_____

_____

Inner critics thrive on perfectionism. What does "perfect" mean to you? In your past, did you feel pressure from others, your culture, or your society to behave, think, feel, or be a certain way? Did others have high expectations of you when you were younger? If so, what were they? What expectation(s) might you have internalized that limit you now? Write down five expectations you have of yourself currently.

1. Expectation: _____

   Is this standard reasonable? _____

   Where did this come from? _____

   If this standard is unrealistic, what would be a more reasonable expectation?

   _____

   _____

2. Expectation: _____

   Is this standard reasonable? _____

   Where did this come from? _____

   If this standard is unrealistic, what would be a more reasonable expectation?

   _____

   _____

3. Expectation: _____

    Is this standard reasonable? _____

    Where did this come from? _____

    If this standard is unrealistic, what would be a more reasonable expectation?

    _____

    _____

4. Expectation: _____

    Is this standard reasonable? _____

    Where did this come from? _____

    If this standard is unrealistic, what would be a more reasonable expectation?

    _____

    _____

5. Expectation: _____

    Is this standard reasonable? _____

    Where did this come from? _____

    If this standard is unrealistic, what would be a more reasonable expectation?

    _____

    _____

When you begin the process of healing, it can be difficult to imagine responding to yourself in the same way you typically respond to a close friend or loved one who is suffering. What kind of challenges do you experience when you try to imagine this?

_____

_____

_____

_____

_____

_____

_____

_____

_____

_____

_____

_____

_____

_____

To have self-compassion, we must first acknowledge our inner critic. For some individuals, self-criticism and self-judgment—also known as our inner critic—come from a specific voice that may have been internalized from the past. Think about your upbringing. Was someone in your life very critical or judgmental? Write down how it was for you to experience them in your life.

_____

_____

_____

_____

_____

_____

_____

_____

_____

_____

_____

_____

_____

_____

Inner critics are notorious for "should have, could have, would have" statements. For example, "I should have done this another way"; "I could have done this differently, and if only I had, I would be better at this." Think about a time when you experienced verbal abuse. Write down any "should have, could have, would have" statements that your inner critic keeps telling you.

_____

_____

_____

_____

_____

_____

_____

_____

_____

_____

_____

_____

_____

_____

Challenging your inner critic takes time, effort, and reminders. Post 10 gentle reminders from the heart on different sticky notes, and place them all around your living space to challenge your inner critic.

1. The way you speak to yourself matters, and I choose to speak to myself with kindness.
2. It's okay to not be okay.
3. I am stronger than I think I am.
4. I am braver than I feel I am.
5. I am doing my best, and I am proud of myself.
6. I am not my thoughts, and I am not my feelings.
7. This is really hard, and I am going to get through this.
8. I know this is painful, and I am more than my pain.
9. I am only human, and I am not alone.
10. I can validate my painful emotions, and I know they will pass.

If you could develop your own gentle reminder and use it as a daily mantra, what would it be?

_____

_____

Self-compassion is a practice of goodwill, not good feelings . . . With self-compassion we mindfully accept that the moment is painful, and embrace ourselves with kindness and care in response, remembering that imperfection is part of the shared human experience.

—KRISTIN NEFF

Research shows that people who experience a high level of self-criticism might feel anxious when learning to be compassionate toward themselves (Warren, 2016). What would it look like to comfort yourself when feelings of fear arise during this learning process? How would you kindly speak to yourself, knowing these feelings are part of this growth process?

_____

_____

_____

_____

_____

_____

_____

_____

_____

_____

_____

_____

_____

_____

When you are in distress, people around you may go into "fix-it" mode, giving unsolicited advice or trying to problem-solve rather than showing care by listening to how you feel. Did your caregivers try to "fix" things when you were feeling uncomfortable feelings? If so, what messages did you receive? What new beliefs can you adopt that refrain from fixing and instead support caring for yourself with compassion?

_____

_____

_____

_____

_____

_____

_____

_____

_____

_____

_____

_____

_____

_____

We're all human, and we all experience feelings of defeat and loss. When we experience continual verbal abuse, it's normal to develop a firm hold on self-hatred, shame, guilt, and anger toward ourselves for letting ourselves down and not knowing what to do. Even after we accept that there are things we cannot change, it can still be challenging to have compassion for our past selves. Write down why you think this might be.

_____

_____

_____

_____

_____

_____

_____

_____

_____

_____

_____

_____

_____

_____

_____

This four-step meditation exercise is a way to show yourself compassion and respond to your inner critic with CARE. Think about an especially challenging time during your experience with verbal abuse—a time when your inner critic was loud as hell. What was it saying, and what were you feeling?

C: Consider the critical thought with a compassionate lens and acknowledge feelings. What critical thought is popping up? What are you currently feeling?

_____

_____

_____

A: Assert a kind response to critical thought and validate feelings. How can you respond to this thought with kindness and acknowledge your feeling?

_____

_____

_____

R: Reinforce a compassionate response with uplifting words to promote self-love. How can you benefit from listening to this kind response?

_____

_____

_____

E: Engage with acts of self-love. What activity can you do now that you enjoy?

_____

_____

_____

As we heal, we're susceptible to feeling regret and doubt, and wishing we'd known better. It's important to remember that we did the best we could; we never could have known exactly what to do. What would it look like for you to meet these experiences and with self-compassion, walk alongside what you cannot change?

_____

_____

_____

_____

_____

_____

_____

_____

_____

_____

_____

_____

_____

_____

Learning self-compassion can be a challenging process. Studies show that some individuals experience fear because it activates the grief associated with feelings of wanting but not receiving affection and care (Warren, 2016). It is incredibly brave to look at such a loss in the search for truth after experiencing the pain of verbal abuse, and it is courageous to then give yourself the love you didn't receive. Write down what comes to mind about the grief of longing. What are different ways you can show yourself grace and self-compassion during moments of grief?

_____

_____

_____

_____

_____

_____

_____

_____

_____

_____

_____

_____

Self-compassion can be an expression of gratitude. Think about the last time you felt grateful. Where were you, and what were you doing? Think about yourself as a person, and list five things that you feel grateful to have in your life right now.

1. _____

2. _____

3. _____

4. _____

5. _____

Coping ahead with kindness is a proactive exercise, inspired by the dialectical behavior therapy (DBT) skill *cope ahead*. This exercise can help prepare you for future situations that previously caused overwhelming feelings and harsh self-judgments. Complete this exercise using a situation that comes to mind, and continue to use this practice to activate self-compassion in situations to come.

1. Describe a future situation that will likely bring forth your inner critic. What feelings will come up, and what will your inner critic be saying to you?

_____

_____

_____

_____

_____

2. Decide how you'll respond to your inner critic, while validating your feelings. What will you say?

_____

_____

_____

_____

_____

3. Make sure you're in a safe space. Close your eyes and imagine the situation as vividly as possible.

_____

_____

_____

_____

_____

4. Rehearse in your mind your response to the situation, coping effectively with kindness.

_____

_____

_____

_____

_____

Kindness can be thoughtful and action oriented. When you feel compassionate, you can show kindness. Think about yourself right now in your recovery journey, and recognize how far you've come. What kinds of things can you tell yourself, coming from a place of kindness? How can you show yourself acts of kindness as you heal?

_____

_____

_____

_____

_____

_____

_____

_____

_____

_____

_____

_____

_____

_____

I am courageously kind to myself through the storms of healing, for I am learning how to sail my ship.

PART 4

RESTORE YOUR SELF-ESTEEM

What lies behind us and what lies before us are tiny matters compared to what lies within us.

—RALPH WALDO EMERSON

Being victimized by verbal abuse can severely erode self-esteem, adversely impacting our everyday lives and causing long-lasting harm to our mental health and our relationships with others. It's normal to have moments of low self-confidence, but enduring continual abuse can create a pervasive and overwhelming sense of inadequacy, uselessness, and deficiency. In this extreme form, low self-esteem can critically strip away our sense of self.

Self-esteem is having confidence in our self-worth, which goes hand in hand with possessing a sense of self-respect. It's about knowing, accepting, and appreciating ourselves. Healthy self-esteem allows us to trust our ability to accomplish goals and overcome hardships, and it gives us the fortitude to help others. The feeling of being comfortable in our own skin allows us to flourish. As we heal from verbal abuse, we can restore a vital sense of self within.

Recognizing your self-worth can be incredibly challenging after experiencing pervasive feelings of worthlessness from verbal abuse. As you admirably embark in rebuilding your self-worth, it's important to remind yourself how far you've come and how this healing process will lead you to the peace you deserve—because you're worth it, and you matter. Knowing your worth is recognizing that you have many wonderful qualities as an individual. Think about these qualities and write down 10 things that make you unique.

1. _____

2. _____

3. _____

4. _____

5. _____

6. _____

7. _____

8. _____

9. _____

10. _____

Erik Erikson, a renowned expert on human development, noted that an important life task for individuals is to achieve a solid sense of self—in other words, a well-defined identity that will lead to a life of consistency, stability, and security (Erikson, 1968). Having a strong sense of self is associated with knowing yourself. Think about yourself in a very honest way. Write down five strengths and five limitations you have.

STRENGTHS

1. _____
2. _____
3. _____
4. _____
5. _____

LIMITATIONS

1. _____
2. _____
3. _____
4. _____
5. _____

When we begin to heal, we start to gain a greater sense of self as well as clarity regarding values that are truly authentic. Engaging in activities driven by intrinsic values can help increase your self-esteem while supporting a sense of control over the experiences that influence your life. How can you integrate more joy into your life? Think about activities you can engage in that will help you in your recovery process. Start by thinking of activities that fit into these categories:

Affiliation with friends, family, and community

_____

Connection with nature

_____

Concern for others

_____

Self-acceptance

_____

Social justice

_____

Creativity

_____

Start very small while you're learning discipline to gradually increase self-respect. What is one small goal you can make to accomplish once a week? Use a small planner or calendar to keep track. In this process, expect resistance, which can take the form of forgetting, or consciously saying to yourself, "I'm over this, I give up." Once this happens, prepare to ruminate.

Ruminating—thinking deeply about something—can lead to spiraling down into a dark abyss of adverse thoughts. When we feel stuck in our thoughts, we can feel paralyzed, incapable of taking reasonable actions that will serve our well-being, and our self-esteem decreases. Fortunately, once we can recognize these thoughts, we can learn to challenge them with practice, and get back up and start again. If you find yourself starting to spiral, refer to this checklist, and ask yourself these questions:How am I feeling?

☐ Am I basing this on facts or feelings?

☐ Is there evidence to support this thought?
  Is there any evidence that contradicts it?

☐ What would a friend say about this?
  What would I tell a friend who had this thought?

☐ Who told me this? Where did I learn this from?

☐ Is this thought helpful to me? Does it help me achieve my goals?

☐ Am I jumping to conclusions?

☐ Will I care about this in a week? In a month? In a year?

Maslow's hierarchy of needs is a theory of mental health proposed by Abraham Maslow. It is based on fulfilling human needs in order of priority, beginning with physiological needs, such as food, water, and sleep, and progressing to self-actualization and achieving one's full potential, such as through creative pursuits. Esteem, which must precede self-actualization, is separated into two categories. The first is esteem for oneself, which includes the need for honor, achievement, mastery, and independence. Think about what esteem for oneself includes, and write down what fulfilling each need would look like, as well as any thoughts and feelings that come up.

_____

_____

_____

_____

_____

_____

_____

_____

_____

_____

_____

_____

When you're building self-respect, you are courageously taking responsibility for your life and your future. Write down what comes to mind and how you feel when you think about responsibility. Consider some benefits and limitations of responsibility. What would it look like for you to take responsibility in your life right now?

_____

_____

_____

_____

_____

_____

_____

_____

_____

_____

_____

_____

_____

_____

Beliefs are what you deem to be true. They can influence what you do and what you don't do. If you believed you were capable of anything—and I mean anything—what would you do tomorrow? What would you do in 5 years or 10 years?

_____

_____

_____

_____

_____

_____

_____

_____

_____

_____

_____

_____

_____

_____

_____

_____

_____

_____

The second category of esteem needs in Maslow's hierarchy of needs is the desire for respect from others. Before we can satisfy this desire, we must learn how to respect ourselves. Self-respect is acknowledging the dignity in yourself, your inherent worth given to you for being born—the birthright of every human being.

Because you exist, it's important for you to hold powerful beliefs about yourself. Get creative and make a birthright poster. Copy onto the poster the following beliefs that you'll learn to internalize. Find a picture of your younger self to put on the poster if you wish. Then place the poster somewhere visible as a gentle reminder throughout your healing process.

I am autonomous.

I am worthy.

I am lovable.

I am powerful.

I am accountable.

I am deserving of respect.

I am deserving of success.

I am deserving of happiness.

I have every right to exist.

I have every right to have fun.

I have every right to thrive.

I have every right to make decisions that serve me.

I have every right to learn from my mistakes.

I have every right to live my life to its fullest potential.

I have every right to ask for and pursue my wants and needs.

I have every right to think for myself.

I have every right to choose my own beliefs.

I have every right to respectfully express myself.

I have every right to validate my own thoughts, feelings, and viewpoints.

I have every right to protect myself.

I have every right to accept myself.

I have every right to accept the things outside of my control.

I have every right to heal and recover.

My life is mine.

My life is significant.

My life is precious.

My life is my responsibility.

All human beings are born worthy.

All human beings are born free.

All human beings are born with equal rights.

All human beings are born without judgment.

The wounded heart learns self-love by first overcoming low self-esteem.
—BELL HOOKS

When we learn to be assertive, many fears can arise around how the person on the receiving end will react or respond. As we address these fears, we gain awareness of what we need to overcome by cultivating courage. To be brave, we must first feel fear. What do you fear when you think about becoming assertive?

_____

_____

_____

_____

_____

_____

_____

_____

_____

_____

_____

_____

_____

_____

Feeling pride is an important ingredient in creating self-confidence. Pride is an emotion that lets us know we've increased our value and worth through the ability to help ourselves and others. Confidence is believing in our abilities. When did you last feel proud and confident?

_____

_____

_____

_____

_____

_____

_____

_____

_____

_____

_____

_____

_____

Humility is a heartfelt kind of confidence that allows you to celebrate accomplishments, recognize your steps forward, acknowledge your shortcomings, and know you are good enough. Shortcomings remind us that no one is perfect and that life is a continual process of learning, improving, growing, and healing, not arriving at a destination. Humility is a state of contentment with yourself, life, and what you can contribute to the world. In what areas of your life do you feel good enough? What areas do you want to grow in?

_____

_____

_____

_____

_____

_____

_____

_____

_____

_____

_____

_____

_____

Identifying your limiting beliefs is important in increasing your sense of self. Limiting beliefs are the stories we tell ourselves that hold us back from becoming who we want to be and doing the things we want to do. Beliefs are incredibly powerful, so it's important to identify those that are untrue and that cause us to feel insecure and powerless.

I feel insecure about _____

because _____.

Underlying limiting belief: _____

Where did this come from? _____

What evidence do you have against this belief? _____

_____

I feel bad about _____

because _____.

Underlying limiting belief: _____

Where did this come from? _____

What evidence do you have against this belief? _____

_____

I can't _____

because _____.

Underlying limiting belief: _____

Where did this come from? _____

What evidence do you have against this belief? _____

_____

I shouldn't _____

because _____.

Underlying limiting belief: _____

Where did this come from? _____

What evidence do you have against this belief? _____

_____

Failure can feel terrifying, especially when we take it personally. When failure is met with harsh criticism, it makes sense that we may want to give up or not even try. Self-esteem increases when we acknowledge that failure is a part of growth—it's success in progress, an experience rather than a testament to our character. Humility reduces self-criticism and lets us learn from our mistakes. Think about failure. What does it mean to you? How can you integrate a supportive mindset and welcome failure as a part of your growth?

_____

_____

_____

_____

_____

_____

_____

_____

_____

_____

_____

Polarized thinking—or all-or-nothing thinking—is a common defense mechanism. It can develop in someone who has experienced continual verbal abuse, and it can be detrimental to self-esteem. You can spot this extreme filter by noting the words "always," "never," "good," and "bad." Think about a time when you felt you failed at something. Describe the situation, the feelings you experienced, and what you told yourself afterward. Circle any "always," "never," "good," and "bad" words you see.

_____

_____

_____

_____

_____

_____

_____

_____

_____

_____

_____

_____

_____

_____

Creating meaningful goals can be a catalyst for increasing self-esteem and pave the way to finding your unique purpose and passion. When we're in the process of healing, it can be hard for us to think of life in a big picture frame, but I assure you that it gets clearer as the journey continues. What is a meaningful goal you can make during your healing process?

_____

_____

_____

_____

_____

_____

_____

_____

_____

_____

_____

_____

_____

Learning to be assertive is essential in rebuilding self-esteem and gaining respect from others. When you're assertive, you're capable of respectfully communicating your needs, asking for what you want, saying no to what doesn't serve you, and standing up for what you believe is right. The 3 Cs of assertive communication can help you be more effective in communicating:

Confidence: *You believe in your ability to handle a situation.*

Clear: *The message you have is clear and easy to understand.*

Controlled: *You deliver information in a calm and controlled manner.*

When you're learning how to be assertive, it can be helpful to practice on your own. Think about a situation in which you would need to be assertive. Stand in front of a mirror. Get into a power pose—that is, stand tall in a position you can associate with power. This is a technique that fosters confidence. Close your eyes and visualize the situation. Now open your eyes and practice communicating assertively using the 3 Cs as guidance.

Small victories are very important for reclaiming your self-esteem. Acknowledging the accomplishment of small steps will increase your capacity for feeling joy and pride. Because pride is an emotion that informs you of an increase in stature, while shame informs you of a decrease in stature, small victories can help combat toxic shame. Write down one small goal you can accomplish by the end of the week, and describe what it would look like for you to celebrate. Warning: Achieving small victories can feel uncomfortable at first, but with time and practice, it will become a valuable lifelong skill.

I possess self-esteem because I know, trust, and respect myself. I am uniquely my own.

PART 5

CONNECT WITH YOUR COMMUNITY

Without community, there is no liberation.

—AUDRE LORDE

After we experience disconnection as a result of verbal abuse, a critical part of the healing process is connecting with others. Finding community among individuals we feel safe with can foster vulnerability, which is a key element in learning how to live authentically as our true selves. This community that you create can provide love, support, acceptance, and a sense of belonging.

Connection can feel impossible after you've endured prolonged verbal abuse. The thought of allowing yourself to become close with another person or group of people can feel daunting at first. If this resonates with you, know that you're not alone. It takes courage to connect with your community. This section will help you reflect on community and encourage you to make the connections that will allow you to not just survive, but thrive.

When you think of the word "community," what comes to mind? What messages did your caregivers, culture, and society give you about community?

_____

_____

_____

_____

_____

_____

_____

_____

_____

_____

_____

_____

_____

_____

_____

_____

Isolation can be a dark consequence of abuse. It involves someone else controlling our attempts to connect with others when we need it most. It's common to experience sadness and feelings of loneliness when isolated. Write down what it looks like for you to feel lonely. How does it affect your day and what you do?

_____

_____

_____

_____

_____

_____

_____

_____

_____

_____

_____

_____

_____

_____

Loneliness can seem like it will last forever, leaving us feeling helpless and depressed. Write about a time when you felt lonely and what it was like. What did you believe at the time? How can you challenge those beliefs, knowing that feelings are temporary, and support yourself in connecting with others?

_____

_____

_____

_____

_____

_____

_____

_____

_____

_____

_____

_____

_____

_____

In DBT, opposite action is a skill that alleviates an intense emotion through the distraction of an action opposing the emotional urge.

1. Identify the emotion (e.g., "I feel lonely").
2. Identify the urge that accompanies the emotion (e.g., "I have the urge to isolate").
3. Identify whether the action urge fits the situation (e.g., "I feel lonely, but that doesn't mean I'm alone").
4. If the action urge doesn't fit the situation, use opposite action (use the options that follow).

For example, sadness is an emotion informing you that you're experiencing a loss. The opposite action to sadness is movement. After you name the feeling, you can tame it by being active. How can you incorporate movement the next time you're feeling a lot of sadness? Write down three things you can do inside and three things you can do outside.

INSIDE

1. _____

2. _____

3. _____

OUTSIDE

1. _____

2. _____

3. _____

Intimacy can be marked as a sense of closeness and connection based on authenticity between two people. Write about what intimacy means to you, including any feelings, thoughts, and beliefs that come up.

_____

_____

_____

_____

_____

_____

_____

_____

_____

_____

_____

_____

_____

_____

_____

Intimacy involves opening up with others, and it can feel scary trying to connect after experiencing continual verbal abuse. Write down what feels scary when you think about opening up to others. How are your fears protecting you at this moment?

_____

_____

_____

_____

_____

_____

_____

_____

_____

_____

_____

_____

_____

_____

_____

_____

_____

Fears around intimacy are often related to experiencing continual disappointment in relationships. Think about your past relationships with people you've trusted and how you've experienced disappointment. How did the disappointment feel? What expectations did others not meet?

_____

_____

_____

_____

_____

_____

_____

_____

_____

_____

_____

_____

_____

_____

In DBT, the opposite action to feeling the emotion of fear is to stay and do what triggers the fear. As we recognize our fears of opening up, we can seek out those we feel the most comfortable with to practice opposite action and become more vulnerable in our healing process. Think about someone you trust, and practice opposite action when talking about your healing process. This can be a trusted friend, family member, or licensed professional therapist.

> **Please note**: *During the early stages of recovery, only practice this skill while opening up with others you know you can trust.*

_____

_____

_____

_____

_____

_____

_____

_____

_____

_____

_____

_____

Alone we can do so little; together we can do so much.
—HELEN KELLER

Connecting to our community involves rebuilding relationships with friends and family. Take some time to evaluate your relationships, and take an honest inventory of who can support you on your healing journey. Write down who listens well, who doesn't interrupt, and who doesn't give advice.

_____

_____

_____

_____

_____

_____

_____

_____

_____

_____

_____

_____

_____

Relationships can become strained as a result of verbal abuse. Write about the relationships you had with others before the abuse, and describe how your relationships were affected.

_____

_____

_____

_____

_____

_____

_____

_____

_____

_____

_____

_____

_____

_____

_____

_____

Reaching out and rebuilding relationships is key in creating sustainable connections. Write down 10 different activities you can do with different people you'd like to foster a relationship with. What would it look like for you to implement those activities with the people you care about during your healing process?

1. _____

2. _____

3. _____

4. _____

5. _____

6. _____

7. _____

8. _____

9. _____

10. _____

Create a Yes List, also known as a Bucket List. Saying yes to new experiences can be helpful in connecting with your community. Think about saying yes to something new. How do you feel, and what thoughts come up? Write down some benefits and limitations of saying yes. Now make a Yes List of 10 new experiences you would like to have in your healing journey.

BENEFITS

1. _____

2. _____

3. _____

LIMITATIONS

1. _____

2. _____

3. _____

YES LIST

1. _____

2. _____

3. _____

4. _____

5. _____

6. _____

7. _____

8. _____

9. _____

10. _____

As you rebuild relationships, it's helpful to strengthen your communication skills. It's common for people recovering from verbal abuse to be conflict-avoidant. Think about how you communicate, and write down what comes to mind when you think of conflict. How would you describe your relationship with conflict and communication?

_____

_____

_____

_____

_____

_____

_____

_____

_____

_____

_____

_____

When we start to connect with others, a fear of commitment can arise. Think about commitment, and write down what comes to mind and what it means to you. What fears come up?

_____

_____

_____

_____

_____

_____

_____

_____

_____

_____

_____

_____

_____

_____

It's important to practice honest and direct communication as you recover from verbal abuse. Think about how you use your voice and how it feels for you to speak your mind. How can you use honest communication to help others? What would it look like to practice honest and direct communication as you heal?

_____

_____

_____

_____

_____

_____

_____

_____

_____

_____

_____

_____

_____

Volunteering your time can be an excellent way to connect with your community. On a larger scale, volunteering at an organization can feel very fulfilling and purposeful, but you can also give back to others in many ways. Think about helping someone out this week. What would that look like? Practice small by volunteering your time to someone close to you.

Recovery from verbal abuse can be incredibly hard to navigate and can often leave you feeling misunderstood. Support groups can be a much-needed resource when you feel the most alone, unable to find someone who can relate to what you're going through. Consider attending a support group for people recovering from verbal abuse, and write down some pros and cons of doing so.

PROS

_____

_____

_____

_____

_____

CONS

_____

_____

_____

_____

_____

I am capable of overcoming
fears and fostering a connection
with my community.

PART 6

COMMIT TO TAKING CARE OF YOURSELF

To love oneself is the beginning of a lifelong romance.

—OSCAR WILDE

Progressing through your healing process requires a commitment to taking care of yourself. Discovering your personal value and capacity for perseverance is one of the greatest expressions of self-love. This personal journey involves an honest understanding of your past, caring for yourself in the present, and accepting responsibility for your future. When you give yourself the care you desire instead of depending on others to provide that care, you begin to reclaim yourself. Self-love is not simply a task to perform, but a new lifestyle to adopt.

Committing to acts of self-care can feel daunting as you walk into an unfamiliar territory of the self. When facing challenges of often crippling self-doubt or self-criticism, you will need to practice methods of patient and gentle inner-guidance. As you progress, you can take satisfaction in your new path of resilient self-love.

When you think about making a commitment to taking care of yourself, what comes to mind? What is scary about this commitment? Write down what could be gained and what could be lost.

_____

_____

_____

_____

_____

_____

_____

_____

_____

_____

_____

_____

_____

_____

Healing is not linear; take your time. Think about what time means in your healing process, and write down any kind of unrealistic expectations you have of yourself. What does it look like to put pressure on yourself? What would it look like to have patience with yourself?

_____

_____

_____

_____

_____

_____

_____

_____

_____

_____

_____

_____

_____

_____

Self-love can mean different things to different people. Write down what self-love means to you. What is your current relationship with self-love? What would you like it to look like in the future?

_____

_____

_____

_____

_____

_____

_____

_____

_____

_____

_____

_____

_____

_____

_____

Learn your self-love language and show yourself some love. Quality time, words of affirmation, physical touch, receiving gifts, and acts of service can be categorized as different ways that someone can express and receive love (Chapman & Summers, 2016). Write down three different ways you can express love to yourself in each language. What would it look like to implement them during your healing process to understand which ones you value the most?

QUALITY TIME

1. _____

2. _____

3. _____

WORDS OF AFFIRMATION

1. _____

2. _____

3. _____

PHYSICAL TOUCH

1. _____

2. _____

3. _____

RECEIVING GIFTS

1. _____

2. _____

3. _____

ACTS OF SERVICE

1. _____

2. _____

3. _____

While you're recovering from verbal abuse, taking care of yourself may feel childish or selfish. Think about your past. When you took care of yourself, was it ever met with criticism or belittlement from others? What messages did you get from your family, culture, or society about self-care? How can you challenge any internalized messages as you learn that self-care is self-love?

_____

_____

_____

_____

_____

_____

_____

_____

_____

_____

_____

_____

_____

As we learn to take care of ourselves, creating routine is important. When you hear the word "routine," what comes to mind? What limiting beliefs do you have about routine that can be challenged? What new beliefs can you adopt to help support sustainable healing?

_____

_____

_____

_____

_____

_____

_____

_____

_____

_____

_____

_____

_____

When we heal, we increase our sense of self and decrease the need to compare ourselves with others. Comparison can trigger emotional fear, highlighting the uncertainty in areas that we feel within ourselves. How does comparison show up in your healing journey? If you discover that you're comparing yourself to others and feeling fear, how can you care for yourself in the moment?

_____

_____

_____

_____

_____

_____

_____

_____

_____

_____

_____

_____

_____

Create a self-love calendar and give yourself daily attention. Checking in with yourself continually can be helpful in creating a foundational support system within and in framing a routine. When you check in with yourself, use this checklist as a guide. (Note: These questions are just to explore self-observation—there's no need to act on anything.)

- ☐ How am I feeling?
- ☐ What emotions am I experiencing?
- ☐ What sensations am I experiencing in my body?
- ☐ What thoughts am I observing?
- ☐ What am I doing currently?
- ☐ What is important to me at this moment?
- ☐ How can I support myself right now?
- ☐ How can I show myself love right now?

Knowing how to be solitary is central to the art of loving. When we can be alone, we can be with others without using them as a means of escape.

—BELL HOOKS

A part of taking care of yourself is asking for help when you need it. What prevents you from asking for help? What kind of messages did you get from your family, culture, or society about asking for help? In times of need, how can you remind yourself that asking for help is an act of self-love?

_____

_____

_____

_____

_____

_____

_____

_____

_____

_____

_____

_____

_____

Healing is about learning and unlearning. What is one thing you've learned during this process that stands out the most? What do you want to learn more about as you continue your journey? What is something you're currently unlearning, and how has that experience been for you? What would you like to unlearn in the future?

_____

_____

_____

_____

_____

_____

_____

_____

_____

_____

_____

_____

_____

_____

_____

Taking care of yourself is a balancing act of supporting and challenging yourself, while also accepting yourself as you are in the moment. What does supporting yourself look like? What does it look like for you to challenge yourself?

_____

_____

_____

_____

_____

_____

_____

_____

_____

_____

_____

_____

_____

_____

_____

Scheduled breaks and rituals are very helpful. Rest is so important when you're taking care of yourself because it helps you recharge and rejuvenate. How would taking a break look for you? Get out your calendar and schedule a resting period during each week.

Social media breaks are also important. Social media is so prevalent these days, and it can cause additional stress. What would doing a social media cleanse look like for you? Think about how you could schedule a social media break, and write it in your calendar.

Self-care rituals are helpful, too. Think about three things you'd like to do on a weekly basis as a ritual. What would they be? Examples are clearing clutter, creating something, engaging in activities that help you rest and recharge, nourishing your body with food or drink, and connecting with nature, your body, or your breath. Schedule these rituals in your calendar.

As we take care of ourselves, it's important to learn how to embrace praise and compliments. What is it like for you to receive compliments from others? How do you usually react? What compliment can you give yourself right now?

_____

_____

_____

_____

_____

_____

_____

_____

_____

_____

_____

_____

_____

_____

_____

When we commit to taking care of ourselves, we recognize longing for the care we think others should give us or have given us. What comes up for you when you think about this? In what ways can you reclaim self-care and learn to care for yourself as you think others should care for you?

_____

_____

_____

_____

_____

_____

_____

_____

_____

_____

_____

_____

_____

_____

_____

When you integrate the harsh realities of the pain you've endured into the story of your life, you are courageously taking care of yourself. Think about holding this truth right now. How are you experiencing this reality? What does this new reality mean to you? How can you care for yourself right now?

_____

_____

_____

_____

_____

_____

_____

_____

_____

_____

_____

_____

_____

_____

A love letter from you to you is a wonderful way to mark growth on your journey to reclaim yourself. Think about making a commitment to take care of yourself now or in the near future. Write a letter to yourself from that place of commitment. What will you call this new chapter in your life? Write the title in the letter's header.

_____

_____

_____

_____

_____

_____

_____

_____

_____

_____

_____

_____

_____

_____

Accountability is a foundational building block of self-love. When people are accountable in taking care of themselves, they can see the bigger picture. They know what needs to be adjusted to foster self-love and take action. What comes to mind when you think about accountability and self-care? How can you build a relationship with accountability during your healing process?

_____

_____

_____

_____

_____

_____

_____

_____

_____

_____

_____

_____

_____

_____

_____

_____

I have the power to take
actions that are aligned with
taking care of myself.

A FINAL WORD

Congratulations! You have made it through this journal, and your bravery deserves to be celebrated! Self-reflection is a tremendously admirable courageous act. Honesty when facing the source of pain fosters peace in recovery.

Contrary to the belief that "time heals all wounds," the most significant aspect of healing is you. Growth can feel like healing and breaking all at once. Sometimes self-care means not being present, and it's okay to require pause. Feelings of apathy and desire for isolation are common. We all experience these moments. We heal in waves and spirals. Just because you're not making progress as quickly as you think you should doesn't mean you're not moving forward. Slowing down is essential in recovery, and it can be the best gift you can give yourself.

As you continue this important work of healing from verbal abuse, remember to choose yourself. When you do this, you create a space to heal and the freedom to explore within. Choose yourself—the rest will come later. You'll create safety within and live comfortably in your own skin. You'll give yourself permission to be real. You'll live by your personal values and endeavor to realize your own dreams, passions, and goals. Through this continuous practice, you're creating a powerful, finely tuned sense of self that is uniquely you, ready to embrace a fulfilling existence while finding a reservoir of hope within community.

Keep in mind that while a continual self-healing journey may work for some, it might not resonate with everyone. If you need help, scheduled therapy from a licensed professional can offer you support and guidance in a structured setting. Healing and recovery does not have a one-size-fits-all treatment, so feel free to experiment with various methods, and always honor what works best for you.

RESOURCES

These national hotline websites provide one-on-one support, safety planning, educational information, support groups, and additional resources. If you are in immediate danger, please call 911.

National Domestic Abuse Hotline: 1-800-799-SAFE (7233) / Text 1-800-787-3224

thehotline.org

Day One: The Call to Safety: 1-866-223-1111

dayoneservices.org/verbal-abuse/

SafeHorizon Abuse Hotline: 1-800-621-HOPE (4673)

safehorizon.org

love is respect Teen Abuse Hotline: 1-866-331-9474

loveisrespect.org

REFERENCES

Carney, Amy, and Russel Neuhart. "Psychological Abuse." *Elder Abuse: Forensic, Legal and Medical Aspects*, edited by Amy Carney, 163–182. London: Academic Press, 2020.

Chapman, Gary, and Amy Summers. *The Five Love Languages: How to Express Heartfelt Commitment to Your Mate*. Nashville, TN: LifeWay Press, 2016.

Ekman, Paul. *Emotions Revealed: Recognizing Faces and Feelings to Improve Communication and Emotional Life*. New York: Henry Holt, 2007.

Erikson, Erik H. *Identity: Youth and Crisis*. New York: W. W. Norton Company, 1968.

Kahneman, Daniel, and Amos Tversky. *Choices, Values, and Frames*. Cambridge: Cambridge University Press, 2017.

Lefler, E. K., and C. M. Hartung. "Disruptive Behaviors and Aggression." *Reference Module in Neuroscience and Biobehavioral Psychology*. 2017. Amsterdam: Elsevier. doi.org/10.1016/B978-0-12-809324-5.06090-9.

Maxwell, John C. *Team 2-in-1: Winning with People and the 17 Indisputable Laws of Teamwork*. Nashville, TN: Thomas Nelson, 2008.

Rizvi, Syeda, Fariha Iram, and Najma Najam. "Parental Psychological Abuse Toward Children and Mental Health Problems in Adolescence." *Pakistan Journal of Medical Sciences* 30, no. 2 (2014). doi:10.12669/pjms.302.4593.

Siegel, Daniel J., and Tina Payne Bryson. *The Whole-Brain Child: 12 Revolutionary Strategies to Nurture Your Child's Developing Mind*. Vancouver, BC: Langara College, 2016.

Warren, Ricks, Elke Smeets, and Kristin Neff. "Self-Criticism and Self-Compassion: Risk and Resilience." December 2016. self-compassion.org/wp-content/uploads/2016/12/Self-Criticism.pdf.

ACKNOWLEDGMENTS

Thank you to my sister, Jessica. I am eternally grateful for your existence, unwavering support, and endless encouragement.

None of this would have been possible without my boyfriend, Eric. Thank you for lending me your brilliant mind and providing me continuous support during this process. I love you.

To my mother, thank you for your endless generosity. I appreciate you and the growth of our relationship.

To my father, I miss you so much. I know you would be proud of me.

A very special thanks to Joe Cho and everyone at Callisto Media for giving me this wonderful opportunity. Thank you to the editorial team for your patience, guidance, and editorial expertise.

Finally, I am not self-made—I am family made, community made, ancestor made. I am made up of everyone I have ever known. Thank you kindly to every person who I've had the pleasure of crossing paths within this lifetime. I am who I am because of you.

ABOUT THE AUTHOR

Stephanie Sandoval, LMFT, is a Latinx licensed marriage and family therapist and the founder of Collective Space Therapy. With extensive training and experience working with individuals experiencing low self-esteem, depression, and trauma, Stephanie provides a creative therapeutic approach to verbal abuse with a humanistic lens. Her practice reflects an active commitment to social justice and intergenerational healing on an individual, community, institutional, and global scale. Stephanie has been a lifelong learner, driven by her innate curiosity and passion for exploration of self and others. With an anti oppressive framework, she holds a vision for providing modern mental health services that reflect the values of ethical and sustainable wellness.

CPSIA information can be obtained
at www.ICGtesting.com
Printed in the USA
BVHW021548140821
614327BV00015B/304